SO-DFI-926

Bill
Cosby

Making America Laugh and Learn

by Harold and Geraldine Woods

DILLON PRESS, INC.   MINNEAPOLIS, MINNESOTA

Library of Congress Cataloging in Publication Data

Woods, Harold.

Bill Cosby, making America laugh and learn.

(Taking part)

SUMMARY: A biography of the comedian and educator, originally from North Philadelphia, who is known as the creator of Fat Albert, Weird Harold, and other characters based on his childhood experiences.

1. Cosby, Bill, 1937-   —Juvenile literature.

2. Comedians—United States—Biography   —Juvenile literature.

[1. Cosby, Bill, 1937-   . 2. Comedians. 3. Educators. 4. Afro-Americans—Biography]

I. Woods, Geraldine. II. Title.

PN2287.C632W6 1983 792.7'028'0924 [B] [92] 82-23497

ISBN 0-87518-240-2

Dillon Press, Inc., 242 Portland Avenue South
Minneapolis, Minnesota 55415

Printed in the United States of America
1 2 3 4 5 6 7 8 9 10 98 97 96 95 94 93 92 91 90 89

The photographs are reproduced through the courtesy of the Brokaw Company, the Children's Television Workshop, SAH Enterprises, and William H. Cosby, Jr., Filmation Associates.

Contents

BILL COSBY

Bill Cosby is one of the most popular and respected stars in show business today. The young boy who grew up playing on the streets of North Philadelphia has made millions of people laugh since he began his career as a comedian in 1962. Fat Albert, Weird Harold, and a host of other characters based on his childhood experiences have become household names. Cosby has starred in award-winning TV shows, acted in several successful movies, and made many best-selling comedy records.

In addition to his show business work, he has earned a Ph.D. in education and has devoted a great deal of time and money to helping people in need. Doctor Cosby uses his education and his skills as an entertainer to teach children all across America. He has starred on the TV series, "The Electric Company," and has appeared on "Sesame Street." Even his cartoon program, "Fat Albert and the Cosby Kids," has an educational message. Speaking about his career, Bill Cosby says that he has pushed himself into many new areas because "In this business, if you stand still, you disappear!"

Bill Cosby tells the story of Noah and the ark.

Introduction

You've probably heard the Bible story about
Noah and his ark. Have you ever wondered what
Noah said when God first spoke to him? Bill
Cosby did. He says Noah was in his workshop,
sawing some wood, when he heard a voice. The
conversation went like this:

> GOD: Noah! I want you to build
> an ark.
>
> NOAH: Right. What's an ark?

Later, Noah has trouble believing that God is
talking to him. He asks, "Who is this, really? Am
I on Candid Camera?" Noah's neighbor is also a
little doubtful when he sees the giant boat:

> NOAH: It's an ark.

NEIGHBOR: Uh huh. You want
to get it out of my driveway?

That's an example of Bill Cosby's imagination.
He wonders about funny things that the rest of us
ignore. Bill is also funny when he talks about his
childhood. Listen to what he says about the time
he and his brother jumped on the bed and broke
it:

FATHER: What's going on in
here?

BILL: A man came in through
the window and started jumpin'
on the bed until it broke.

FATHER: There's no window in
this room.

BILL: He brought it with him!

If you laughed when you read that, you're not
alone. Since he started his career as a comedian
in 1962, Bill Cosby has made millions of people
laugh. Bill has starred in award-winning televi-

sion shows, acted in several popular movies, and made many best-selling records. And he's not only a comedian. He has also earned a doctorate in education—the highest degree a university can give. And even though he has a very busy schedule, Bill has always found time for charity. He has spent many hours and a lot of money helping needy people all across the country.

These are just a few reasons why Bill Cosby is one of the most popular entertainers in America. But he wasn't always a famous man. As Bill himself says on one of his records, "I started out as a child."

1. "I started out as a child"

William Henry Cosby, Jr., was born at three o'clock in the morning on July 12, 1937. His parents were Anna and William Cosby. The Cosbys lived in a small apartment in North Philadelphia, Pennsylvania.

Just about everyone in Bill's neighborhood was black, and most were poor. The Cosbys were a little better off than some of their neighbors. Bill and his younger brothers James, Russell, and Robert always had enough to eat. Their clothes were not the best, but they were clean and warm.

Like many others in their neighborhood, though, the Cosbys did have some hard times.

Bill's brother James was often very sick. When Bill was eight, James died.

Another problem was Bill's father, who once had held a good job. Sadly, he lost that job and had to take another one at lower pay. Soon after James' death, Bill's father left to join the Navy.

Bill's mother was someone Bill could always depend on. When her husband left, Anna Cosby took a job as a maid. She worked twelve hours a day or more to provide for her family. Even that was not always enough. At times, the Cosbys had to go on welfare.

Bill remembers one Christmas when the family didn't have enough money for a Christmas tree. He took an orange crate and painted it bright colors. Then he put a little Santa Claus on top. Bill thought his "tree" would cheer everyone up. However, when his mother saw the crate, she knew her boys missed having a real tree. Somehow, she managed to save enough money to buy a small tree and a few presents. Looking back on those days, she says the only thing she had to give Bill was plenty of love.

Anna Cosby really gave her son more than love. "As a boy," Bill remembers, "my mother used to read Mark Twain [a famous American writer] to me...I was impressed with his fantastic sense of humor." From Twain, Bill picked up some tips on how to tell a good story. That helped him later when he began to write stories for his comedy act.

Bill's mother was his first and best audience. She loved to listen to his jokes, and she encouraged him to tell funny stories.

Anna Cosby also taught her son right from wrong. When Bill was bad, she always cried. That made Bill cry, and behave better. He says now that he never wanted to do anything really wrong because he never wanted to embarrass his mother.

As a young boy, Bill picked up some tips on how to tell a good story from Mark Twain.

Although he was only nine, Bill became the man of the house when his father left. He tried to help his mother by getting a job. Taking some rags and polish, he went downtown to shine shoes. Two years later, at age eleven, Bill spent his summer as a stockboy in a grocery store. He worked from six in the morning until six at night, with extra hours on weekends. For all that effort, he earned only eight dollars a week. Bill also had a job dusting and cleaning in a local drugstore.

Working hard didn't keep Bill from enjoying himself. Whenever he could, he went out to play with his friends. They called Bill "Cos" or "Cool Cos." Cos and his pals had a good time, even though his neighborhood didn't have many parks and yards. In fact, Bill claims he didn't know there was dirt under the cement until he was all grown up!

The boys played baseball, basketball, and football. Bill, who is a natural athlete, sharpened his sports skills during these games. Today, in his comedy routines, he likes to tell stories about his early adventures.

One of the funniest explains how Bill and the gang played football on a city street. The quarterback gave these instructions to his team: "Arnie, go down ten steps and cut left behind the black Chevy. Filbert, you run down to my house and wait in the living room. Cosby, you go down to Third Street and catch the J bus, have him open the doors at Nineteenth Street and I'll fake her to ya."

2. "He should grow up to do great things"

When Bill wasn't playing with his friends or working, he went to Wister Elementary School in Philadelphia. Though he was a smart child, Bill was much more interested in clowning around than he was in learning his lessons. As Bill says, "I found I could make people laugh, and I enjoyed doing it...I thought that if people laughed at what you said, that meant they liked you. Telling funny stories became, for me, a way of making friends."

Unfortunately, Bill's teachers did not always approve of his jokes. Also, his clowning sometimes kept him from learning. His early report cards contain many poor marks.

Luckily, Bill's fifth and sixth grade teacher, Mary Forchic Nagle, understood his need to perform. She gave him parts in school plays. The future star acted in "King Koko from Kookoo Island," "Back to the Simple Life," and "Tom Tit Tot."

Mary Nagle knew that there was something special about Bill. On one of his report cards she wrote, "William is a boy's boy, an all around fellow, and he should grow up to do great things."

However, even Mrs. Nagle sometimes lost patience with the class clown. Another time she wrote, "In this classroom there is one comedian and it is I. If you want to be one, grow up, get your own stage, and get paid for it." She probably never dreamed that her young student would follow her advice and become a world famous entertainer!

Bill got good grades in Mrs. Nagle's class. He also did well in other ways while at Wister. He was captain of the baseball and track teams, and president of his class.

After Wister, Bill went on to Fitz-Simons Junior High and Central High School. Central High accepted only the best students. The classes were difficult, and the students had to study hard to keep up with the work. Bill, however, was only interested in sports and having fun. He failed many of his subjects, and finally transferred to Germantown High School.

Bill (kneeling, second row, second from left) *with other members of the Central High School football team in Philadelphia in 1953.*

At Germantown the work was easier, but that didn't help Bill much. Again, he couldn't keep his mind on his studies. And again, he spent most of his time and energy on sports. Bill was the captain of Germantown's football and track teams, and a star athlete.

In class Cos tried to be a star also. He clowned around a lot, and quickly became, as he says, "the class nut." Too much play and too little work made Bill fail. He was left back once, in the tenth grade. Finally, he dropped out of school.

Bill found out that there aren't many interesting jobs for people without an education. He worked in a shoe repair shop for a while, but he found the job very boring. At times he put high heels on men's shoes just to amuse himself! Bill says that both he and the owner of the store agreed that he should get another job.

Bill did get another job, in a car muffler plant. But he quickly realized that it was no better than shoe repair. Bill began to understand that he had to get a grip on his future. To get away from the dead-end jobs, in 1956 he enlisted in the United States Navy.

Bill stayed in the navy for four years. While he was a sailor, he grew up into a serious young man with a purpose in life. Of course, he still clowned around and made people laugh, and he also kept up his interest in sports.

Bill finally understood that there could be room for both play and work in his life. He studied hard and received a high school diploma. Then the Navy assigned him to a hospital where he worked with sick and crippled sailors. Bill enjoyed helping people, and he was good at his job.

However, Bill knew he didn't want to stay in the navy forever. He also knew that unless he had more education, he would have to take another dead-end job.

At last Bill decided to go to college and become

As a star athlete on the Temple University track team, Bill competed in many events. Here he is preparing to throw the shot for the shot put.

a gym teacher. Since he had no money to pay for college, he applied for a scholarship. Temple University in Philadelphia thought that Bill's sports skills could help their teams. They offered him a four-year athletic scholarship, on the condition that he keep his grades up.

So, at the age of 23, Bill left the navy and became a college student at Temple. At last he had his life in order. He enjoyed dating and parties with his friends, and he played on the basketball, football, and track teams. Most importantly, he earned good grades.

Bill was so good at sports that he might have made a career as a pro football player. He might have become everybody's favorite gym teacher, too. However, things didn't work out quite that way for William Henry Cosby, Jr. Life had a surprise in store for him.

3. "You'd better have plenty of guts"

Bill recalls that he wanted to do something crazy the summer after his second year at Temple. He needed a job because his scholarship didn't cover his day-to-day living expenses. But what kind of a job?

Bill decided to be a bartender. He found a job at a small café in Philadelphia called "The Underground." When Bill made drinks for people, he added an extra ingredient—laughter.

Before long the owner of The Underground noticed that Bill was serving funny stories along with the cocktails. He offered him a job as a comedian. Bill said yes, though he had not intended to get into show business.

A stand-up comic is an entertainer who stands in front of a microphone and tells jokes. At "The Cellar"—the room in The Underground where Bill performed—Cool Cos became the world's first *sit down* stand-up comic. The Cellar was so tiny that it had no stage. Instead, Bill did his act on a table. Since his height didn't allow him to stand up, Bill had to sit on a chair placed on top of the table. And the only way he could reach his performing place was by climbing over the bar!

At first, Bill used stories and jokes written by other comedians. He also told racial jokes— stories about blacks and whites and the differences between them. Before long, though, he decided to concentrate on other things.

Bill believes that people should learn to understand one another better, and he thinks his comedy can help to make that happen. As he says: "Rather than trying to bring the races of people together by talking about the differences,

Bill Cosby believes that his comedy can help people of all races to understand one another better and show what they have in common.

let's try and bring them together by talking about the similarities [the things that are the same]." Bill hopes that by laughing together, black and white people will come together as friends.

To carry out his ideas, Bill used stories from his childhood in his comedy act. He changed many of the stories a little to make them funnier. Still, his act was based on real experiences—experiences that people of all races share.

A good example of Bill's comedy is his story about monsters. Who hasn't been afraid of monsters at one time or another? Bill told his audiences that when he was very young, six monsters lived in his bedroom closet. They would wait until all the lights were out and then sneak into the room. Bill would yell, "Help! Monsters!" His mother would scream, "Get out of here!" The monsters would go away, and Bill's life would be saved. His father was a little different. He would say, "OK. Let them eat you up!"

Bill told another story about a bottle of water his family kept in the refrigerator for cold drinks. When he was too lazy to fill the bottle, he would put it back in the refrigerator with just a little bit left. Talking about this part of his act, Bill says: "The situations I talk about, people can find themselves in...it makes them glad to know they're not the only ones [who do these things]. For example, how many of us have put the ice water bottle back in the refrigerator with just enough water left so we don't have to refill it? Be honest now."

Bill also told his audiences about his boyhood pals. Again, he took real people and added some imagination to their stories. One friend was Fat Albert, who weighed two thousand pounds and shouted "Hey Hey Hey" wherever he went. According to Bill, bricks fell off buildings whenever Fat Albert walked down the street!

Another pal was Weird Harold, who was sup-

*Fat Albert and the Cosby Kids became the stars
of their own TV show.*

posed to be six feet, nine inches tall and as skinny as a toothpick. Bill told his audiences that he and Weird Harold liked to go to monster movies together. They never saw any monsters, though, because they were too scared to look at the screen!

Dumb Donald, Crying Charlie, and other friends were also part of Bill's act. These characters became very popular. Years later Bill made cartoons and comic strips about their adventures.

Bill made his stories even funnier with weird sound effects. *Whoopa whoopa* was Noah sawing wood for his ark. *Pkhhh* was a gunshot he fired from his two fingers when he was a kid, and *Thuph* was the same gunshot when one of his fingers had a bandaid on it.

Bill's sound effects made his stories even funnier.

Audiences enjoyed Bill's funny stories. Before long, Bill began to receive job offers from other clubs. He even appeared on television. His summer job was turning into a full-time career.

Now Bill had an important decision to make. He knew he couldn't stay at Temple and also be a comedian. There just wouldn't be enough time for study, sports, and work. He also knew that "breaking into show business is one of the hardest...longest...most discouraging things you can do. If you want to make the...try, you'd better have plenty of guts and determination..."

In the middle of his third year at Temple, Bill decided that he did have the guts to succeed as a comedian. He dropped out of school and, as he says, "the struggle was on."

4. "Bill Cosby is a very funny fellow, right"

After he left Temple, Bill's career really started to take off. He played to bigger audiences at more popular clubs, and received better pay. He also made a best-selling comedy album, "Bill Cosby Is A Very Funny Fellow, Right!" Bill began to travel across the country, performing in San Francisco, Chicago, New York, and other cities.

During his comedy act, Bill told his audiences how he discovered girls: "You're out there playing ball, and one day the ball no longer looks as good as the girl." One day in 1963, Bill discovered a very special young woman.

It happened while Bill was working in Washington, D.C. A friend suggested that he take a student from the University of Maryland on a date. The student's name was Camille Hanks. She was young, pretty, and fun to be with. Bill and Camille went bowling, and by the end of the evening, Bill says, he knew he wanted to marry her.

The young comedian and college student carried on a long-distance romance. Bill had to return to New York to work at a club called "The Bitter End." His last show ended at four o'clock in the morning. Bill would sleep until nine, and then drive to Camille's house in Maryland. They would spend a few hours together, though sometimes Bill fell asleep at the movies! Then Bill would drive back to New York in time to go to work. He was always tired because of this busy schedule.

After four or five dates, Bill asked Camille to marry him. She said yes. Her parents, however, were not happy about the match. Camille's father and mother were worried about Bill's future. In their eyes, Bill was a dropout who was trying for a career in a very risky business. They told Camille to break her engagement.

Camille did as her parents asked—for a while. But soon the couple got back together again, and this time the romance was too strong to be broken off. Bill and Camille were married on January 25, 1964.

In that same year, Bill branched out into another part of show business—acting. A starring role in a new television series called "I Spy" was offered to him. It was a challenge. As Bill says, "It was so completely different from anything I had ever known. Storytelling is one thing, but playing a definite character...and serious yet ...that's something else."

Bill took the part of Alexander Scott, a tennis coach who traveled around the world with a player, Kelly Robinson. Scotty and Kelly, though, were really spies. Week after week they battled master criminals and had many hair-raising adventures.

"I Spy" made television history. Until it appeared, blacks were shown on television only in second-rate roles—as maids, chauffeurs, and the like. But there was nothing second-rate about Alexander Scott. He was supposed to be a brilliant man who spoke seven languages. In every way he was the equal of Kelly, who was played by white actor Robert Culp. Like Bill's comedy routines, "I Spy" highlighted what people of all races have in common. It showed a black man and a white man living and working together as close friends.

"I Spy" was a great success, and so was Bill. The show stayed on the air for four years. Bill received an Emmy award for best actor in three of those years. An Emmy is like an Oscar, but it is given for TV programs instead of for movies.

As Alexander Scott, the brilliant spy on the TV show "I Spy," Bill Cosby won three Emmy awards.

When "I Spy" went off the air, Bill starred in several TV variety shows. His first special program won an Emmy. He also acted in a few comedy series. In one he played the part of Chet Kincaid, a gym teacher. That was the career Bill thought he was preparing for when he first went to Temple!

While Bill was on TV, he continued to record comedy albums. He won six Grammy awards for his work. A Grammy is the record industry's highest honor.

Bill also became a movie star. He acted in a movie called *Man and Boy,* which was about the time after the Civil War. He starred in *Uptown Saturday Night* and *Let's Do It Again* with his friend Sidney Poitier. Another pal, Robert Culp from the "I Spy" show, acted with Bill in the film *Hickey and Boggs.* Bill starred in the movie version of *California Suite,* too.

In the early 1980s, Bill added still another

activity to his busy schedule. He began appearing in many commercials advertising such products as computers, vegetables, Jell-O, and Kodak film. Somehow, Bill also found the time to form a jazz band called Badfoot Brown and the Bunions Bradford Funeral and Marching Band.

Bill once said about his career, "I was quite satisfied with my work after I got going." With the success of his latest project, "The Cosby Show," he should be even more satisfied today!

5. *"If you stand still, you disappear."*

In the summer of 1983, Bill began working on his most successful TV series yet. He had decided he wanted to make a television show about an American family. Bill thought that there was too much violence and crime on TV at the time; he thought people needed something better to watch.

Bill created "The Cosby Show." It is a story about a family very much like Bill's own family. Heathcliff Huxtable—played by Bill—and his wife, Claire, live in a nice home in New York City. "Cliff" is a doctor and Claire is a lawyer, and they have five children—Sondra, Denise, Theo, Vanessa, and Rudy. The TV show deals with day-to-day life in an average family. The children have problems with dating, homework, chores, and with each other. Cliff and Claire have problems with work and with the children. The Huxtables are the type of family that solves problems by talking with each other, not yelling.

"The Cosby Show" was voted the best program on television for three years in a row, and has won many awards. Bill even won another Emmy for his work on the show. He was right about what Americans wanted to watch on TV!

Bill says the show is popular because it is not about a black family or a white family. It is about an American family that happens to be black. Bill doesn't believe in pointing out people's differences. Instead, he thinks people get along much better when they know how much they share—and they all share problems that come with being a part of a family.

"The Cosby Show" was so successful, Bill decided to create another TV show, called "A Dif-

Bill Cosby (back) *and his TV "family" on the set of "The Cosby Show."*

ferent World." At first, it was about one of the Huxtable children, Denise, and the problems she faced when she left home and went to college. Today, the show is about more than one person. It is a series that many people like because they see themselves in the characters, just as in "The Cosby Show."

Besides working on two television series, Bill has written two books. With so many children of his own, and because he spends a lot of time on TV playing a father, Bill decided to write a book about what it is like to raise children. He called it *Fatherhood*. It was a big success, and brought Bill a lot of attention. In 1987, he wrote another book, *Time Flies*, about what it is like to get old. Both books are funny, but they also have important messages in them.

Bill has also continued to make records for both children and adults, and in 1987, he starred in another film, *Leonard Part 6*.

With his busy schedule, Bill spends a lot of time flying around the country, but as he once said himself, "I know it's hard to keep pushing yourself into different areas, but you have to if you want to be around in a few years. In this business, if you stand still, you disappear!"

6. "Honesty, character, dignity."

Work isn't the only thing in Bill Cosby's life. First and most important is his family. Bill and Camille are the parents of five children, including four daughters—Erika, Erin, Ensa, and Evin— and one son, Ennis. The Cosby family has homes in Manhattan (a part of New York City), Philadelphia, and Los Angeles. They spend most of their time, though, at a large, old house in Amherst, Massachusetts. Camille Cosby has made a comfortable home there for her busy family.

Bill is a loving father. When his children were very young, Camille would take the babies and travel with Bill. Once the Cosby children reached school age, however, they had to stay at home.

Bill and Camille Cosby (front, center) *with four of their children and some young friends.*

Yet Camille says that Bill really knows and understands each of his children. Cos has a very special relationship with all children. This is because he believes, "If you listen to what a child is saying to you carefully, you'll see that...he has a point to make. So I listen. And I answer them just as seriously as possible. And if I don't know the answer, I'll tell them I don't know."

Bill Cosby is also a strict parent. According to him, the *e* in each of his children's names stands for *excellent*. That's exactly what he expects his children to be. He wants his son and daughters to work hard and achieve as much as they are able to. In fact, he once complained to the school that his kids didn't get enough homework!

Bill considers education a valuable part of life. Even after he became a successful comedian, Bill continued to study and learn. He went back to college and received a doctorate in education. A doctorate is the highest degree that a university gives to its students. Bill is now entitled to be called "Dr. Bill Cosby." He was even elected a trustee of Temple University—not bad for a former dropout!

Two of Bill's children, Erin and Ennis, both

attended colleges in the South, and Bill hopes that his other children will continue their educations after high school, too.

Because Cos feels education is so important, he donated $20 million to Spelman College, the school Erin went to, so it could build a new academic center for students and professors. The center will be called the Camille Olivia Hanks Cosby Academic Center, after Bill's wife.

In addition to this donation to the college, Bill shows his support of many other organizations and charities. He has helped the American Sickle Cell Foundation, the Black Film Foundation, the mentally retarded, the Hemophilia Foundation, and other groups. Sometimes he gives money, and sometimes he donates his time for a good cause. He has played in many tennis tournaments to raise money.

Bill thinks it is important to help people. While he was working on his doctorate, "Dr. Cosby" studied the use of television and other electronic ways of educating children. He doesn't, however, intend to be a classroom teacher. Instead, he uses his skills as an entertainer to teach children all across America.

For many years, Bill starred in the educational TV series, "The Electric Company." "The Electric Company" teaches children to read better by sounding out words. It makes learning fun by surrounding it with comedy, music, and dance. Bill also appeared on "Sesame Street," teaching counting and letters to younger children.

His cartoons, such as "Fat Albert and the Cosby Kids," have an educational message, too. In one show, for example, Dumb Donald has a new baby sister. He isn't too happy about it at first. However, he finally grows to understand that his sister is part of his family. He is even proud of her!

Bill does these kinds of shows because, as he

Bill Cosby entertained millions of children in "The Electric Company's" award-winning reading series.

says, "I'm interested in just one thing. Poor white kids and poor black kids...Someone has to help these kids in there." Bill also says, "These teachers, they need a lot of help, you know."

Bill has tried to help kids in other ways, too. He made a record called "Bill Cosby Talks to Kids About Drugs." It warns young people about the dangers of heroin, speed, and other drugs.

Bill himself doesn't drink or use drugs of any kind. He hopes the record will get the message across: "Overindulgence (using too much of) anything is the wrong way, but when you're talking about hard drugs—heroin, speed, that stuff—you're talking about a way that can only lead to the end of the road. Even if you're lucky, and the end of the road is only a hospital, think of the time out of your life to recover. Every person I have ever known who had developed a bad habit spent most of the rest of his life trying to kick it, staying with it, or never using it forever...The time spent acquiring a drug habit and kicking it is time kids could have used to educate themselves." Bill has some thoughts about drugs in the black community: "A junkie never caused freedom for any people."

As an entertainer, educator, and a family man, Bill Cosby, the poor boy from Philadelphia, has certainly come a long way. Yet he wants to travel even farther; he doesn't want to "disappear."

Bill has certainly not done that. His career has grown like a sturdy tree since his first comedy job in The Cellar more than twenty-five years ago. Instead of disappearing, he has become more popular than ever.

Bill has been growing as a person, too. He says, "I am trying to live my own life in a way that I feel is very difficult, but I also find it very rewarding in that I treat each and every individual according to what he sounds like, and what his response is to me and what my response is to

him." In other words, Bill believes in being straight and honest to every person, whether that person is black, white, young, or old.

Bill also thinks that "honesty, character, dignity, and how much one respects the other individual" are the best ways to judge the true worth of a person.

If William Henry Cosby, Jr., is judged that way, he turns out to be a fantastic human being!

At the age of 52, Dr. Bill Cosby is one of the most popular entertainers in America.

Index

The Authors

Harold and Geraldine Woods are the authors of
many books for young people. The Woods have a
special interest in the needs and skills of the
students in America's inner cities, for they teach
remedial reading and writing at Saint Jean Baptiste
High School in New York City.

This biography is especially important for inner
city and minority students, the authors believe,
because "Bill Cosby encountered many obstacles—
poverty, an absent father, troubles in school—and
overcame them all. More than an entertainer, he is
an example to young people trying to face problems
in their own lives." The Woods hope that telling Bill
Cosby's story may help young people with similar
problems to deal with them in a way that will enrich
and enhance their own lives and the lives of others
in their communities.